The Adventures of B

i CAN TiE MY SHOES

Written by: Chris Simms
Illustrated by: Courtney Farmer

"Time to get ready to go," Mom says. Bella and William grab their shoes.

They're running to get their shoes.

"Bella got back first, so I'm going to tie her shoes first," Mom said.

Mom is tying Bella's shoe.
William is watching.

"Your turn, William. Let me tie your shoe for you." Mom said. William says, "I can do it!"

William is trying to tie his shoe.

Good job, William! You tied your shoe.

Bella looks down and his shoes are not tied. They're tucked into his shoes.

"We're at the playground, kids!" Mom says.

Yay! They both jump out of the car.

"William, your shoe is loose,"
Bella says.
"Okay, I will tie it." He replies.

Bella turns to look as he ties his shoes.

"William? I do not think that's the right way." Bella says.

William grabs Bella by the hand as they run off to play again.

'William! Be careful, your shoe strings!"
William tripped on his shoelaces.

William starts crying out for
mom.
"MOM!"

"Your shoe may not have been tied tight enough. I'll re-tie them for you," Mom says.

"Mom, maybe I still need your help with tying my shoes." William says.

"I'll always be here for you when you need me," Mom says.

"Don't worry, William, we will learn to tie our shoes together," Bella says.

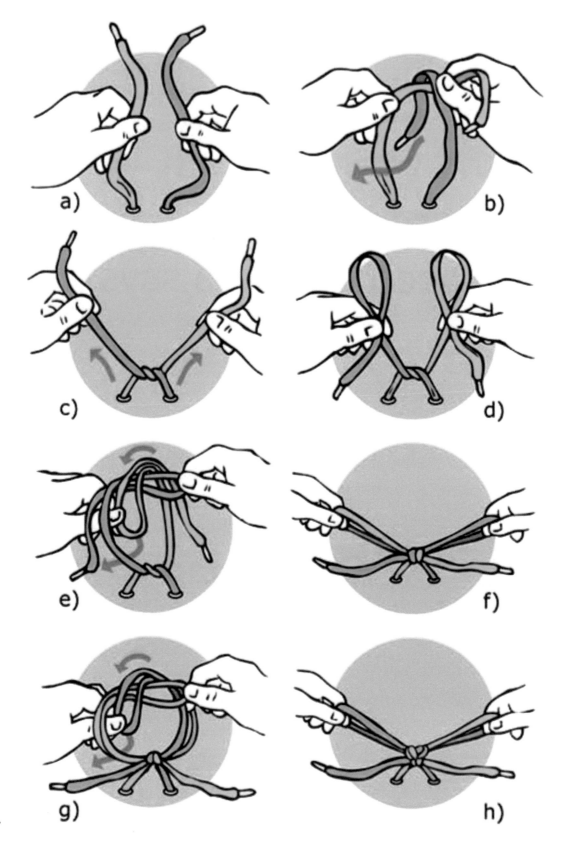

Made in the USA
Columbia, SC
13 August 2024

40456113R00027